THE **7** HABITS

"At some time in your life, you probably had someone believe in you when you didn't believe in yourself."

—Stephen R. Covey,
The 7 Habits of Highly Effective People

THE 7 HABITS OF HIGHLY EFFECTIVE

Graduates

SEAN COVEY

Inspired by the Wisdom of Stephen R. Covey

For permission requests, please contact the publisher at:
Mango Publishing Group
2850 S Douglas Road, 4th Floor
Coral Gables, FL 33134 USA
info@mango.bz

For special orders, quantity sales, course adoptions and corporate sales, please email the publisher at sales@mango.bz. For trade and wholesale sales, please contact Ingram Publisher Services at customer.service@ingramcontent.com or +1.800.509.4887.

The 7 Habits of Highly Effective Graduates

ISBN: (p) 978-1-64250-920-5 (e) 978-1-64250-921-2
BISAC: SEL027000 SELF-HELP/Personal Growth/Success

Printed in the United States of America

Table of Contents

Congrats Grad!

Welcome to the rest of your life.
Now that you have graduated, endless
opportunities await. What comes next?
Discovering what's important to you, planning
your next steps, and deciding what you want to
contribute to the world can seem daunting. But
with the wisdom and thoughtful questions in this
card deck, you will be inspired toward effectiveness
and success. Every week, read a section and reflect
upon the lesson and question. Take this book with
you on-the-go so you will use it often. Let these
messages and quotes from my father's bestselling
book, *The 7 Habits of Highly Effective People*,
inspire you and get you thinking about how
you want to live your life.
The future is yours.
Best of luck!

Sean Covey

What Are the 7 Habits?

Habit 1: Be Proactive
Take responsibility for your life. You are not a victim of genetics, circumstance, or upbringing. Live life from your Circle of Influence.

Habit 2: Begin with the End in Mind
Define your values, mission, and goals.
Live based upon your vision of your life.

Habit 3: Put First Things First
Prioritize your activities and focus on what matters most. Spend more of your time on matters that are important but not urgent.

Habit 4: Think Win-Win
Have an everyone-can-win attitude; be happy for the success of others.

Habit 5: Seek First to Understand, Then to Be Understood
Listen to people empathically and then ask to be heard.

Habit 6: Synergize
Value and celebrate differences so that you can achieve more than you ever could have alone.

Habit 7: Sharpen the Saw
Consistently recharge your batteries in all four dimensions: physical, mental, spiritual, and social/emotional.

INTRODUCTION

Which

Habit

calls to you the most?

INTRODUCTION

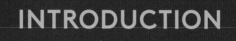 *If you*

apply even one
of the 7 Habits
today, you can see
immediate results;
it's a lifetime
adventure—a life
promise.

INTRODUCTION

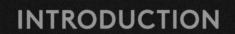

Is there

something you've always wanted to
change about yourself?

INTRODUCTION

People

who live by their ethics
have strong roots, deep
roots. They withstand
the stresses of life, and
they keep growing and
progressing.

INTRODUCTION

focused on quick fixes at the
expense of your character?

INTRODUCTION

 want to make minor changes in your life, work on your behavior. But if you want to make significant, quantum breakthroughs, work on your paradigms.

INTRODUCTION

How

accurate are your paradigms, or
perceptions of the way things are?

INTRODUCTION

 *Between*

what happens to us
and our response is
a space, and the key
to our growth and
happiness is how we
use that space.

INTRODUCTION

How

could you respond proactively
the next time you face a highly
charged situation?

INTRODUCTION

A

Transition Person

is one "who breaks unhealthy, harmful, abusive or unfortunate learned behaviors and replaces them with proactive, helpful, effective behaviors. This person models positive behaviors and passes on effective habits that strengthen and build others in positive ways."

INTRODUCTION

Who

has been a Transition Person
for you? What influence did
they have on your life?

HABIT

1

BE PROACTIVE

"A serious problem with reactive language is that it becomes a self-fulfilling prophecy. People... feel victimized and out of control, not in charge of their life or their destiny. They blame outside forces—other people, circumstances, even the stars—for their own situation."

Are

your words making
you a victim?

1

BE PROACTIVE

"I am not the product
of my circumstances.
I am a product of my
decisions."

1

BE PROACTIVE

How

differently do you feel
about yourself when you
use proactive language?

1

BE PROACTIVE

"Be a light, not a judge.
Be a model, not a critic."

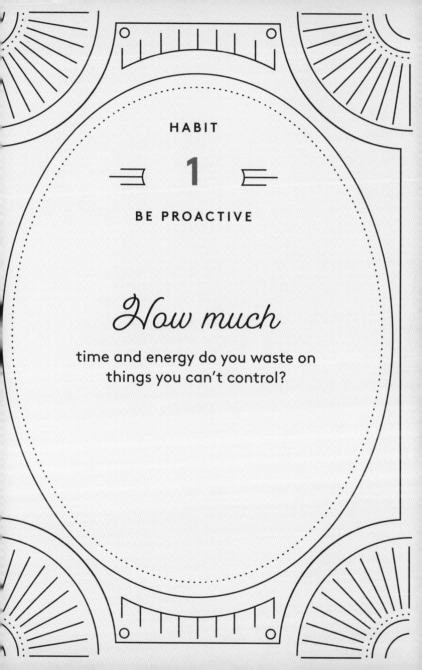

HABIT

1

BE PROACTIVE

How much

time and energy do you waste on
things you can't control?

HABIT

1

BE PROACTIVE

"Proactive people focus their
efforts on the Circle of Influence.
Their energy is positive, enlarging,
and magnifying."

1

BE PROACTIVE

Is your

Circle of Influence—the
sum of things you can
control—growing
or shrinking?

1

BE PROACTIVE

"Every human being has four endowments—self-awareness, conscience, independent will, and creative imagination. These give us the ultimate human freedom: the power to choose."

≡ **1** ≡

What

decision that only you can make
have you been putting off?

2

BEGIN WITH THE
END IN MIND

"It's incredibly easy to work harder and harder at climbing the ladder of success, only to discover that it's leaning against the wrong wall."

How are

your outcomes different when you
begin with a clear end in mind?

2

BEGIN WITH THE END IN MIND

"Deep within each one of us
is an inner longing to live a life of
greatness and contribution—to really
matter, to really make a difference."

HABIT

2

BEGIN WITH THE
END IN MIND

What

legacy do you
want to leave?

2

BEGIN WITH THE END IN MIND

"The mission statement gives you a changeless sense of who you are."

2

BEGIN WITH THE END IN MIND

What is

the compelling vision, or
mission statement, of your future?

To build your own mission
statement, please visit
https://msb.franklincovey.com/

2

BEGIN WITH THE END IN MIND

"How different our lives are when we really know what is deeply important to us."

HABIT

2

BEGIN WITH THE
END IN MIND

This week,

how can you tend to a relationship
that matters most to you?

2

BEGIN WITH THE END IN MIND

"We detect rather than invent our missions in life."
—Viktor Frankl

Which

people in your life are most
affected by your personal mission?

2

BEGIN WITH THE END IN MIND

"One of the major problems that arises when people work to become more effective in life is that they... lose the sense of proportion, the balance...they may neglect the most precious relationships in their lives."

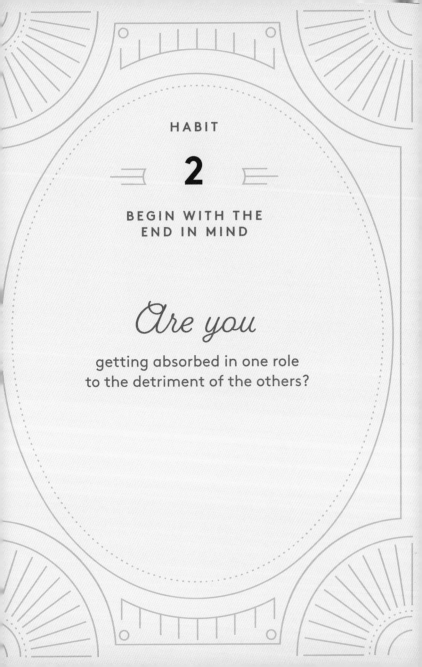

HABIT

2

BEGIN WITH THE END IN MIND

Are you

getting absorbed in one role
to the detriment of the others?

3

PUT FIRST THINGS FIRST

"Happiness—in part—is the fruit of
the desire and ability to sacrifice
what we want now for
what we want eventually."

What

one thing can you do that, if done
regularly, would make a tremendous,
positive influence on your life?

"The key is not to prioritize what's on your schedule, but to schedule your priorities."

HABIT

3

PUT FIRST THINGS FIRST

Q1 Necessity

Crises
Emergency meetings
Last-minute deadlines
Pressing problems

Q2 Effectiveness

Proactive work
Important goals
Planning and prevention
Relationship building

Q3 Distraction

Needless interruption
Irrelevant meetings
Unimportant
communications
Others' minor issues

Q4 Waste

Trivial work
Avoidance activites
Excessive downtime, TV,
gaming, gossiping, etc.

Which

quadrant do you spend most
of your time in? What are the
consequences?

3

PUT FIRST THINGS FIRST

"Most of us spend too much time
on what is urgent and not enough time
on what is important."

HABIT

3

PUT FIRST THINGS FIRST

How many

of your crises could be
prevented with preparation?

3

PUT FIRST THINGS FIRST

"The main thing is to keep the main thing *the main thing*."

HABIT

3

PUT FIRST THINGS FIRST

Q1 Necessity

Crises
Emergency meetings
Last-minute deadlines
Pressing problems

Q2 Effectiveness

Proactive work
Important goals
Planning and prevention
Relationship building

Q3 Distraction

Needless interruption
Irrelevant meetings
Unimportant
communications
Others' minor issues

Q4 Waste

Trivial work
Avoidance activites
Excessive downtime, TV,
gaming, gossiping, etc.

Which

Q2 activity do you most
need to implement?

3

PUT FIRST THINGS FIRST

"If you were to ask me what single practice would do more than any other to balance your life and increase your productivity, it would be this: Plan your week... before the week begins."

HABIT

3

PUT FIRST THINGS FIRST

What

are the one or two most important
things you can do in each of your
roles this week?

3

PUT FIRST THINGS FIRST

"As you go through your week...
the urgent but not important will
threaten to overpower the important
Quadrant 2 activities you planned.
Use your independent will
and maintain your integrity to
the truly important."

HABIT

3

$\equiv$ ⫦⫣ $\equiv$

PUT FIRST THINGS FIRST

What

pulls you away from following
through on your most important
priorities? How do you feel when you
give in to pressure and neglect them?

3

PUT FIRST THINGS FIRST

"You have to decide what
your highest priorities are and
have the courage—pleasantly,
unapologetically—to say 'no' to other
things. And the way you do that is by
having a bigger 'yes' burning inside."

HABIT

3

PUT FIRST THINGS FIRST

Q1 Necessity

Crises
Emergency meetings
Last-minute deadlines
Pressing problem

Q2 Effectiveness

Proactive work
Important goals
Planning and prevention
Relationship building

Q3 Distraction

Needless interruption
Irrelevant meetings
Unimportant
communications
Others' minor issues

Q4 Waste

Trivial work
Avoidance activites
Excessive downtime, TV,
gaming, gossiping, etc.

How much time are you
spending in Quadrants 3 and 4?
What price are you paying to
stay there?

"Make a little promise to yourself
and keep it; then a little bigger one,
then a bigger one. Eventually, your
sense of honor will become greater
than your moods."

HABIT

3

PUT FIRST THINGS FIRST

Do you

trust yourself to follow through
on the commitments you
make to yourself?

PRIVATE VICTORY
TO
PUBLIC VICTORY

"In relationships,
the little things
are the big things."

If your

relationships were bank accounts,
do you know what constitutes
withdrawals and deposits for the
important people in your life?

PRIVATE VICTORY
TO
PUBLIC VICTORY

"To rebuild broken relationships,
we must first study our own
hearts to discover our own
responsibilities, our own faults."

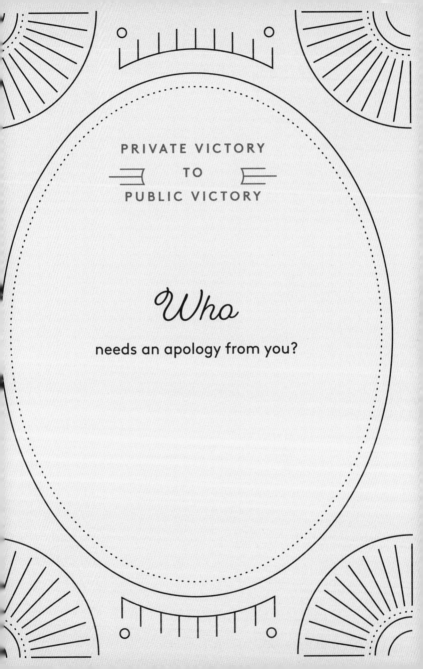

PRIVATE VICTORY

TO

PUBLIC VICTORY

Who

needs an apology from you?

PRIVATE VICTORY
TO
PUBLIC VICTORY

"Any time we think the problem
is 'out there,' that very thought is
the problem."

PRIVATE VICTORY

TO

PUBLIC VICTORY

Are you

carrying around the burden of
someone else's words or actions?

4

THINK WIN-WIN

"Win-Win is not a technique;
it's a total philosophy of human
interaction. It is a frame of mind
and heart that seeks mutual benefit
in all interactions. Win-Win sees
life as a cooperative, not a
competitive, arena."

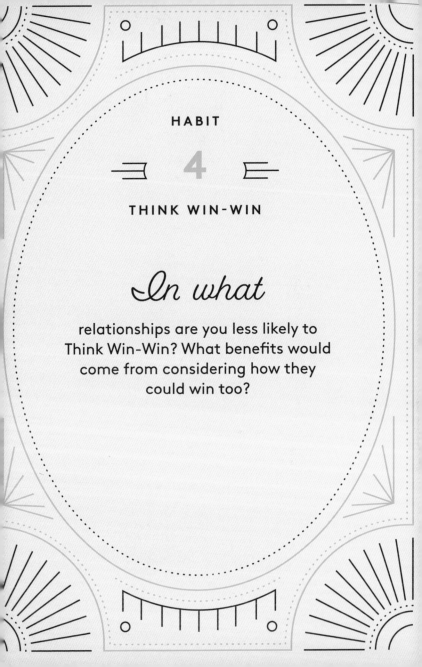

HABIT

4

THINK WIN-WIN

In what

relationships are you less likely to
Think Win-Win? What benefits would
come from considering how they
could win too?

4

THINK WIN-WIN

"Most people are deeply scripted in the Scarcity Mentality. They see life as having only so much, as though there were only one pie out there. And if someone else gets a big piece of pie, it means less for everybody else."

Where does

a Scarcity Mentality show up the most in your life? What negative impacts have you noticed in this way of thinking?

4

THINK WIN-WIN

"The Abundance Mentality flows out
of a deep inner sense of personal
worth and security. It is the paradigm
that there is plenty out there and
enough for everybody."

HABIT

4

THINK WIN-WIN

Do you

truly believe that there is more than enough for everyone?

"If people can express their feelings and convictions with courage balanced with consideration for the feelings and convictions of others, they are mature, particularly if the issue is very important to both parties."

4

THINK WIN-WIN

Are there

relationships in which you lack
courage or consideration? What price
are you paying?

HABIT

4

THINK WIN-WIN

"An agreement means very little in
letter without the character and
relationship to sustain it in spirit.
We need to approach Win-Win from
a genuine desire to invest in the
relationships that make it possible."

HABIT

4

THINK WIN-WIN

What is

your intent when you negotiate with
others? Are you committed to Win-Win?

4

THINK WIN-WIN

"It's amazing how much you can accomplish when it doesn't matter who gets the credit."
—Harry S. Truman

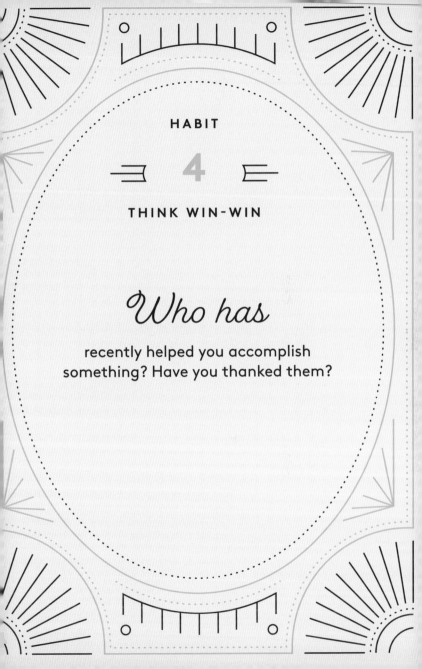

HABIT

4

THINK WIN-WIN

Who has

recently helped you accomplish
something? Have you thanked them?

5

SEEK FIRST TO UNDERSTAND, THEN TO BE UNDERSTOOD

"Next to human survival, the greatest need of a human being is psychological survival—to be understood, to be affirmed, to be validated, to be appreciated."

5

SEEK FIRST TO UNDERSTAND, THEN TO BE UNDERSTOOD

Do people

around you feel that you genuinely
understand them?

5

SEEK FIRST TO UNDERSTAND, THEN TO BE UNDERSTOOD

"When you really listen to another person from their point of view, and reflect back to them that understanding, it's like giving them emotional oxygen."

HABIT

5

SEEK FIRST TO UNDERSTAND, THEN TO BE UNDERSTOOD

Are you

truly listening to those you love?

5

SEEK FIRST TO UNDERSTAND, THEN TO BE UNDERSTOOD

"Listen, or your tongue will
make you deaf."
—Native American Proverb

5

SEEK FIRST TO UNDERSTAND, THEN TO BE UNDERSTOOD

Do you

listen with the intent to reply, rather than to understand?

5

SEEK FIRST TO UNDERSTAND, THEN TO BE UNDERSTOOD

"When you present your own ideas clearly in the context of a deep understanding of the other person's paradigms and concerns, you increase the credibility of your ideas."

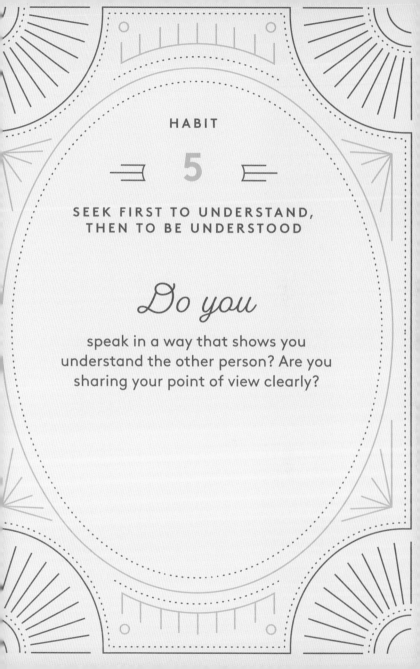

HABIT

5

SEEK FIRST TO UNDERSTAND,
THEN TO BE UNDERSTOOD

Do you

speak in a way that shows you
understand the other person? Are you
sharing your point of view clearly?

5

SEEK FIRST TO UNDERSTAND, THEN TO BE UNDERSTOOD

"*Empathy* is the fastest form of human communication."

5

SEEK FIRST TO UNDERSTAND, THEN TO BE UNDERSTOOD

How

can you listen with empathy during
text, phone, and email conversations?

6

SYNERGIZE

"Insecure people have a need to mold others into their own thinking. They don't realize that the very strength of the relationship is in having another point of view. Sameness is uncreative—and boring."

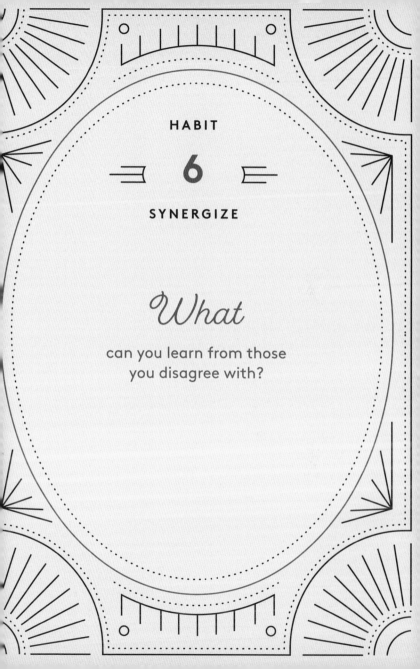

HABIT

6

SYNERGIZE

What

can you learn from those
you disagree with?

6

SYNERGIZE

"Alone we can do so little;
together we can do so much."
—Helen Keller

In which

situations can I practice
synergy today?

"What is synergy? Simply defined, it means that the whole is greater than the sum of its parts. Synergy means that one plus one may equal ten, or a hundred, or even a thousand!"

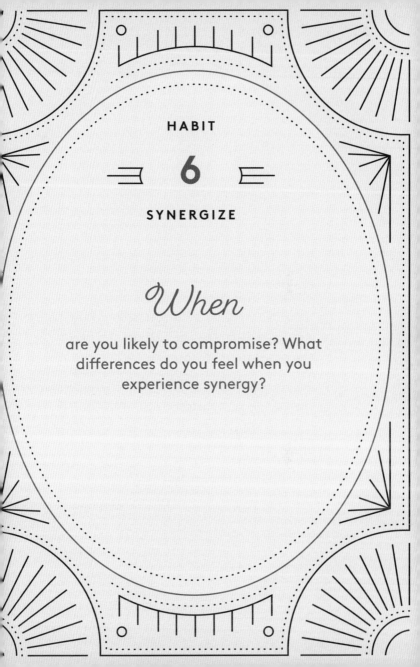

HABIT

6

SYNERGIZE

When

are you likely to compromise? What differences do you feel when you experience synergy?

6

SYNERGIZE

"The essence of synergy is to value
differences—to respect them, to build
on strengths, to compensate for
weaknesses."

Do you know

the unique strengths of the people you work and live with? In which relationships do you tolerate differences rather than value them?

"The key to valuing differences is to realize that all people see the world, not as it is, but as they are."

Are you

open to learning from differences?

HABIT

 6

SYNERGIZE

"When you introduce synergy...you unfreeze (restraining forces), loosen them up, and create new insights."

6

How

can seeking another point of view
help you overcome a seemingly
insurmountable obstacle?

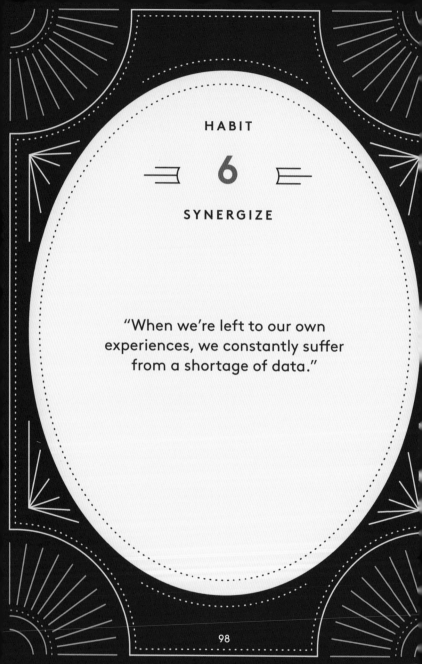

HABIT

6

SYNERGIZE

"When we're left to our own experiences, we constantly suffer from a shortage of data."

HABIT

6

SYNERGIZE

What

could you do to take greater
advantage of the strengths of
others in your life?

HABIT

7

SHARPEN THE SAW

"This is the single most powerful investment we can ever make in life—investment in ourselves, in the only instrument we have with which to deal with life and to contribute."

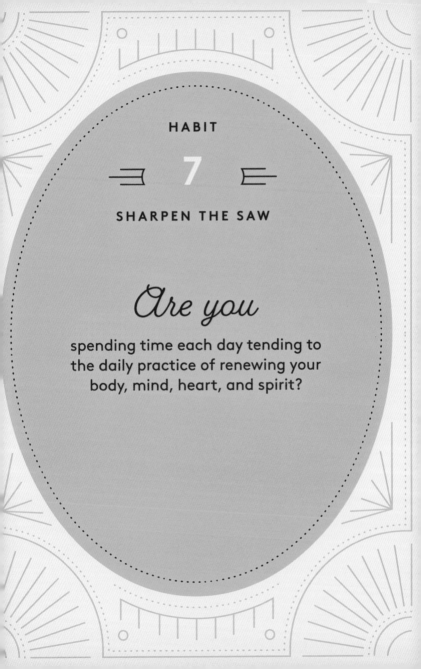

HABIT

7

SHARPEN THE SAW

Are you

spending time each day tending to
the daily practice of renewing your
body, mind, heart, and spirit?

HABIT

SHARPEN THE SAW

"Most of us think we don't have enough time to exercise. What a distorted paradigm! We don't have time not to."

What's

one way you could improve your
physical strength and resilience?

7

SHARPEN THE SAW

"The spiritual dimension is your core, your center, your commitment to your value system."

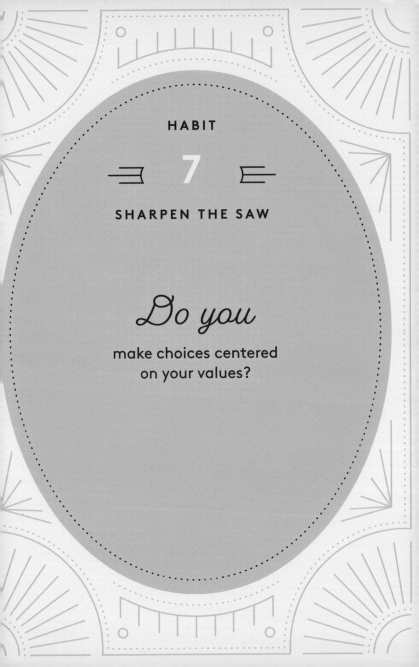

HABIT

7

SHARPEN THE SAW

Do you

make choices centered
on your values?

7

SHARPEN THE SAW

"There's no better way to inform and expand your mind on a regular basis than to get into the habit of reading good literature."

7

SHARPEN THE SAW

Do you

begin the week mentally refreshed?

7

SHARPEN THE SAW

"To touch the soul of another human
being is to walk on holy ground."

Who

can, and should, you emotionally
connect with this week?

7

SHARPEN THE SAW

"This is the single most powerful
investment we can ever make in life—
investment in ourselves."

7

SHARPEN THE SAW

Are

"urgencies" crowding out
your renewal time?

7

SHARPEN THE SAW

"For all our efforts to manage our time, do more, be more, and achieve greater efficiency through the wonders of modern technology, why is it we often find ourselves in the 'thick of thin things'?"

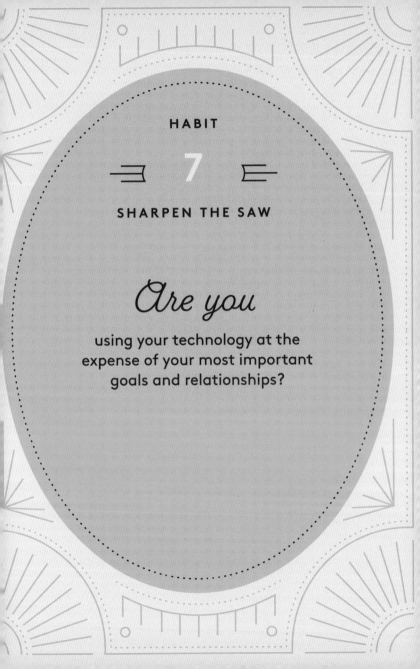

HABIT

7

SHARPEN THE SAW

Are you

using your technology at the
expense of your most important
goals and relationships?

Bonus
Features

Mission Statement Builder

"How different our lives are when we really know what is deeply important to us, and, keeping that picture in mind, we manage ourselves each day to be and to do what really matters most."

—Stephen R. Covey

As I debated on what bonus features to add to this book, I asked myself, "What will have the greatest influence on my reader and on their future?" And then I remembered when my colleague, Annie, once shared this story:

> "I taught the 7 Habits at a local community college for several years. It was an incredible experience helping these young people, and not-so-young, non-traditional students, about the power of habits, goals, and principles. As their teacher and friend, I was curious about the impact of the content and the habits on the students. I wanted to know where they felt the greatest connection and the greatest return on their time by taking this class. So, I randomly added a 'freebie' question to the final exam. I wanted to give the students an opportunity to share honestly—and every test should include a freebie question, shouldn't it?

No one should totally fail every question on a test unless they simply don't take it.

"The question at the end of the final exam was, 'What is your favorite habit and why?' I was very surprised to discover that an overwhelming majority of the students chose Habit 2: Begin with the End in Mind. The reasons varied, but a central theme came through: this was the first time most of these students had plotted out a course for their future. Some, not all, had plotted a course for college and what they wanted to study and embrace as a profession, but many were in college only because it was expected. About 99 percent of my college students had no life vision—no driving purpose, no life contribution, no life mission.

"I was totally stunned when semester after semester, my students voiced the same thing at the end of the course—'I NOW finally have a purpose and meaning to my life.'

"I think I was so surprised because I had chosen my life goals at a young age—I don't know why or what drove me to focus on goals, but somehow I did and just assumed that everyone else did, too."

This experience is likely not uncommon. There are many who have not specifically defined what contribution they want to make in life, or what their driving purpose will be. For this reason, I felt it important to provide a means of doing this. Even if you have defined your life goals at an earlier time, like Annie, this could be an exercise that reinspires you to stay on track. Who knows? Your goals might even change.

Please enjoy the following thoughts and ideas and, as you read, ask yourself these questions:

- Have I defined my purpose in life?
- Am I aware of what I uniquely can do that others can't or won't do?
- What and who do I want to be in my life?
- What principles and values do I want to live my life by?
- What will be my legacy?

To fill this out digitally, visit https://msb.franklincovey.com/missions.

Use everything you learned in this book to help you build your mission statement and become the most effective person you can be. Your effectiveness can change the world.

———————

THE EDITOR

"Writing or reviewing a mission statement changes you because it forces you to think through your priorities deeply, carefully, and to align your behavior with your beliefs. As you do, other people begin to sense that you're not being driven by everything that happens to you."

—Stephen R. Covey

Visualize Your Legacy

Before we get to the mission statement-building questionnaire, please find a place to read these next few pages where you can be alone and uninterrupted. Clear your mind of everything except what you will read and what I will invite you to do.

In your mind's eye, see yourself going to your 80th birthday party. You see the faces of friends and family as they raise their champagne glasses to drink to your continued heath. You feel the care and history that radiates from the hearts of the people there.

As you walk down to the front of the room and prepare to thank everyone for coming, it suddenly sinks in. This is your 80th birthday! All these people have come to honor you. As you wait for the cake to be brought out, you look around and see there are four people lined up to make a speech.

The first is from your family. The second speaker is one of your friends. The third speaker is from your work. And the fourth is from your community.

Now think deeply. What would you like each of these speakers to say about you and your life?

"If you carefully consider what you wanted to be said of you in the funeral experience, you will find your definition of success."

If you participated seriously in this visualization experience, you touched for a moment on some of your deep, fundamental values. You established brief contact with that inner guidance system.

...

To Begin with the End in Mind means to start with a clear understanding of your destination. It means knowing where you're going so that you better understand where you are now and so that the steps you take are always in the right direction. This is something I once wrote about this habit:

"Habit 2, Begin with the End in Mind, means developing a clear picture of where you want to go with your life. It means deciding what your values are and setting goals. If Habit 1 says you are the driver of your life, Habit 2 says decide where you want to go and draw up a map to get there."

How different our lives are when we really know what is deeply important to us, and, keeping that picture in mind, we manage ourselves each day to be and to do what matters most.

We each have a number of different roles in our lives—different areas or capacities in which we have responsibility. I may, for example, have a role as an individual, a husband, a father, a teacher, and a businessman. And each of these roles is important.

One of the major problems that arises when people work to become more effective in life is that they don't think broadly enough. They lose the sense of proportion, the balance, the natural ecology necessary to effective living. They may get consumed by work and neglect personal health. In the name of professional success, they may neglect the most precious relationships in their lives.

You may find that your mission statement will be much more balanced and much easier to work with, if you break it down into the specific role area of your life and the goals you want to accomplish in each other.

Writing your mission in terms of the important roles in your life gives you balance and harmony.

It keeps each role clearly before you. You can review your roles frequently to make sure that you don't get totally absorbed by one role to the exclusion of others that are equally or even more important in your life.

After you identify your various roles, then you can think about the long-term goals you want to accomplish in each of those roles. We're into the right brain, using imagination, creativity, conscience, and inspiration. If these goals are the extension of a mission statement based on correct principles, they will be vitally different from the goals people normally set. They will be in harmony with correct principles, with natural laws, which gives you greater power to achieve them. They are not someone else's goals you have absorbed. They are your goals. They reflect your deepest values, your unique talent, your sense of mission.

> "I think each of us has an internal monitor or sense, a conscience, that gives us an awareness of our own uniqueness and the singular contributions we can make."

An effective goal focuses primarily on results rather than activity. It identifies where you want to be, and, in the process, helps you determine where you are.

Roles and goals give structure and organized direction to your personal mission. If you don't yet have a personal mission statement, it's a good place to begin. Simply identify the various areas of your life and the two or three important results you feel you should accomplish in each area to move ahead; this will give you an overall perspective of your life and a sense of direction.

STEPHEN R. COVEY

...

FranklinCovey's personal mission statement builder will help you create a unique, personalized mission statement. To build your own Personal Mission Statement online, visit msb.franklincovey.com.

Let's begin.

Mission Statement Questionnaire

There are journaling pages at the end of this section to jot down your answers, take notes, and reflect on anything you've learned.

Step 1: Performance
1) I am at my best when…

2) I am at my worst when…

Step 2: Passion
1) What do I really love to do at work?

2) What do I really love to do in my personal life?

Step 3: Talents
1) My natural talents and gifts are: (Examples may be art, music, decision-making, being a friend, etc.)

Step 4: Imagination
If I had unlimited time and resources, and knew I could not fail, what would I choose to do?

1) I would:

Step 5: Vision
Imagine your life as an epic journey with you as the hero/heroine of the story. What do you imagine your journey to be about? Complete the following statement by describing what you are doing, who is it for, why you are doing it, and what the journey's results are.

1) My life's journey is...

Step 6: Character
1) Imagine your 80th birthday. Who will be there with you? What tribute statement would you like them to make about your life?

Step 7: Contribution
1) What do I consider to be my most important future contribution to the most important people in my life?

Step 8: Conscience
1) Are there things I feel I really should do or change, even though I may have dismissed such thoughts many times? What are they?

Step 9: Influence

Imagine you could invite to dinner three people who have influenced you the most—past or present. Write their names in the boxes below. Then record the one quality or attribute you admire most in these people.

1) Name:

1) Attribute:

2) Name:

2) Attribute:

3) Name:

3) Attribute:

Step 10: Balance

Let's think of balance as a state of fulfillment and renewal in each of the four dimensions: physical, spiritual, mental, and social/emotional. What is the single most important thing you can do in each of these areas that will have the greatest positive impact on your life and help you achieve a sense of balance?

1) Physical:

2) Spiritual:

3) Mental:

4) Social/Emotional:

Over the years, your circumstances will change. Your priorities will change. Your goals and dreams will change. That's okay—because change means growth. As you grow, transform, and broaden your horizons, allow yourself the freedom to expand and refine your mission statement.

For now, congratulate yourself on a job well done. Tell your friends about your newly stated purpose in life.

The next step is learning how to live your mission. Maybe it's easy, but maybe it takes some guidance. We're here to help. Learn more about our classes and training here: www.franklincovey.com/tc/publicworkshops.

Life is a journey. And your mission statement is your map.

Inspiring Thoughts on Missions and Goals

"Your mission statement becomes your constitution, the solid expression of your vision and values. It becomes the criterion by which you measure everything else in your life."

—Stephen R. Covey

"To the person who does not know where he wants to go there is no favorable wind."

—Seneca

"My mission in life is not merely to survive, but to thrive; and to do so with some passion, some compassion, some humor, and some style."

—Maya Angelou

"If you're proactive you don't have to wait for circumstances or other people to create perspective-expanding experiences. You can consciously create your own."

—Stephen R. Covey

"Personal leadership is not a singular experience. It doesn't begin or end with the writing of a personal mission statement. It is, rather, the ongoing process of keeping your vision and values before you and aligning your life to be congruent with those most important things."

—Stephen R. Covey

"Stay focused on the mission."

—Naveen Jain

"Here is a test to find whether your mission on Earth is finished: If you're alive, it isn't."

—Richard Bach

"A mission statement is not something you write overnight. It takes deep introspection, careful analysis, thoughtful expression, and often many rewrites to produce it in final form. It may take you several weeks or even months before you feel really comfortable with it, before you feel it is a complete and concise expression of your innermost values and directions."

—Stephen R. Covey

"Would you tell me, please, which way I ought to go from here?" "That depends a good deal on where you want to get to," said the Cat. "I don't much care where—" said Alice. "Then it doesn't matter which way you go," said the Cat.

—Lewis Carroll, *Alice in Wonderland*

"I've always been inspired by women, and my mission was to inspire women. I always wanted to become a certain kind of woman, and I became that woman through fashion. It was a dialogue. I would see that the wrap dress made those women confident, and made them act with confidence."

—Diane von Furstenberg

"How different our lives are when we really know what is deeply important to us, and keeping that picture in mind, we manage ourselves each day to be and to do what really matters most."

—Stephen R. Covey

"A personal mission statement is like
a tree with deep roots. It is stable
and isn't going anywhere but it is also
alive and continually growing."

—Sean Covey

"The bigger your mission becomes, the
greater inspiration you will be given."

—Ryuho Okawa

"Personal leadership is not a singular
experience. It doesn't begin or end with the
writing of a personal mission statement.
It is, rather, the ongoing process of
keeping your vision and values before you
and aligning your life to be congruent
with those most important things."

—Stephen R. Covey

Affirmations on the Go

Here are some affirmations to keep you focused on your mission, and remind you of the power of the habits. As you work on each habit, take one of these affirmations and repeat it to yourself throughout the day. Make it your focus, and watch your perspective change.

Habit 1: Be Proactive

My ability to conquer my challenges is limitless; my potential to succeed is infinite.

I wake up every morning feeling positive and enthusiastic about life.

I carry my own weather.

I am mindful of my language. I avoid reactive language.

I face my failures head-on. The only failure is giving up. I learn from my failures.

I recognize resistance as merely an obstacle, not a roadblock.

I face my fears head on. I learn from them.

I push pause and think before reacting to an emotional or difficult situation.

Habit 2: Begin with the End in Mind

I am willing to explore new and uncharted territory.

I am the architect of my life; I build its foundation and choose its contents.

I live by my mission. I follow the beat of my inner drummer. I will be myself, not what others want me to be.

I invest my time, talents, abilities, and life in those activities which fulfill my ultimate purpose.

I am the captain of my ship; I chart my own course and choose my own cargo.

I refer back to my mission statement whenever I am faced with important life decisions.

I frequently ask myself: "Is the life I'm living leading me in the right direction?"

Habit 3: Put First Things First

My mind is energized, clear, and focused on the process of my goals.

My daily goals will ensure I reach my long term goals.

For today, I am truly attentive to my work. I will be observant and attentive throughout the day.

Today I will spend time strengthening relationships.

I turn my dreams into goals. I turn my goals into steps. I turn my steps into actions. I complete an action every day.

I will prepare today for future crises.

I concentrate all my efforts on the things I want to accomplish in life.

I spend my time focused on what matters most.

Habit 4: Think Win-Win

I face difficult situations with a balance of courage and consideration. I will find solutions in these difficult times.

In seeking for Win-Win I focus on the issues, not the personalities or positions.

I am genuinely happy for the success of others.

My abundance mentality flows out of my own deep inner sense of personal worth and security.

I choose a Win-Win frame of mind and heart that constantly seeks mutual benefit in all human interaction.

I confidently practice Win-Win as a habit of interpersonal leadership.

When others are scripted in Win-Lose, I balance courage with consideration in finding mutual benefit.

Habit 5: Seek First to Understand, Then to Be Understood

I listen reflectively without judgment to gain complete understanding.

I choose to see things from another's point of view before sharing my own.

The deepest need of the human heart is to be understood.

I listen with my heart, my eyes, and then my ears.

I show my level of care and commitment by empathically listening.

I am mindful of timing and my choice of words when I give feedback.

I practice patience and understanding with others and myself.

Habit 6: Synergize

I am a problem solver. I work with others to find the very best solutions.

I celebrate diversity and I value differences in people and ideas.

In my personal relationships, I strive for the ideal environment for synergy—a high emotional bank account, think Win-Win, and seek first to understand.

I am committed to working with others to create a better solution.

I keep my mind open to the possibilities of teamwork and communication.

There is an abundance of benefit, recognition, and success to go around for everyone.

Habit 7: Sharpen the Saw

I am fit, healthy, and full of self-confidence. My outer self is matched by my inner well-being.

I have strength in my heart and clarity in my mind.

I seek balance in the four dimensions of my life: physical, mental, spiritual, and social/emotional.

I am calm and relaxed which energizes my whole being.

Life is an upward spiral of learn, commit, do, and learn, commit, and do over and over again.

My body is a marvelous machine. I handle it with care and I don't abuse it.

I look for ways to build others up rather than to tear them down.

I find peace and calm in nature.

I use my gift of imagination to clearly visualize the attainment of my goals.

7 Quick Takeaways from The 7 Habits on the Go

Habit 1: Be Proactive. Take responsibility for your life. You are not a victim of genetics, circumstance, or upbringing. Live life from your Circle of Influence.

Habit 2: Begin With the End in Mind. Define your values, mission, and goals in life. Live life based upon your vision of your life.

Habit 3: Put First Things First. Spend more of your time in Quadrant II: the quadrant of important but not urgent.

Habit 4: Think Win-Win. Have an everyone-can-win attitude; be happy for the success of others.

Habit 5: Seek First to Understand, Then to Be Understood. Listen to people empathically and then ask to be heard.

Habit 6: Synergize. Value and celebrate differences so that you can achieve more than you ever could have alone.

Habit 7: Sharpen the Saw. Consistently recharge your batteries in all four dimensions: physical, mental, spiritual, and social/emotional.

ABOUT
SEAN COVEY

Sean Covey is a business executive, author, speaker,
and innovator. He is President of FranklinCovey Education and
is devoted to transforming education throughout the world.
Sean oversees FranklinCovey's whole school transformation
process, called Leader in Me, which is now in over 4,000 schools
and 50 countries throughout the world.

Sean is a *New York Times* bestselling author and has authored or
coauthored several books, including the *Wall Street Journal* #1 Business Bestseller,
*The 4 Disciplines of Execution, The 6 Most Important Decisions You'll Ever Make,
The 7 Habits of Happy Kids, The Leader in Me,* and *The 7 Habits of Highly Effective
Teens,* which has been translated into 30 languages and sold over 5 million copies
worldwide. He is a versatile keynoter who regularly speaks to youth and adults.

Sean graduated with honors from BYU with a Bachelor's degree in
English and later earned his MBA from Harvard Business School.
As the starting quarterback for BYU, he led his team to two bowl
games and was twice selected as the ESPN Most Valuable
Player of the Game.

Sean and his family founded and run a global, nonprofit
charity called Bridle Up Hope whose mission is to inspire hope,
confidence, and resilience in at-risk young women
through equestrian training.

Sean and his wife, Rebecca, live with their
children in Alpine, Utah.

ABOUT
STEPHEN R. COVEY

Dr. Stephen R. Covey passed away in 2012, leaving behind
an unmatched legacy of teachings about leadership, time
management, effectiveness, success, and love and family. A
multimillion-copy bestselling author of self-help and business
classics, Dr. Covey strove to help readers recognize the principles
that would lead them to personal and professional effectiveness.
His seminal work, *The 7 Habits of Highly Effective People*,
transformed the way people think and act upon their problems
with a compelling, logical, and well-defined process.

As an internationally respected leadership authority, family expert,
teacher, organizational consultant, and author, his advice gives
insight to millions. He sold more than thirty million books (in fifty
languages), and *The 7 Habits of Highly Effective People* was named
the #1 Most Influential Business Book of the Twentieth Century. He
was the author of *The 3rd Alternative, The 8th Habit, The Leader in
Me, First Things First,* and many other titles. He held an MBA from
Harvard and a doctorate from Brigham Young University.
He lived with his wife and family in Utah.

FranklinCovey
ALL ACCESS PASS

The FranklinCovey All Access Pass provides unlimited access to our best-in-class content and solutions, allowing you to expand your reach, achieve your business objectives, and sustainably impact performance across your organization.

AS A PASSHOLDER, YOU CAN:

*   Access FranklinCovey's world-class content, whenever and wherever you need it, including *The 7 Habits of Highly Effective People®: Signature Edition 4.0, Leading at the Speed of Trust®*, and *The 5 Choices to Extraordinary Productivity®*.

*   Certify your internal facilitators to teach our content, deploy FranklinCovey consultants, or use digital content to reach your learners with the behavior-changing content you require.

*   Have access to a certified implementation specialist who will help design impact journeys for behavior change.

*   Organize FranklinCovey content around your specific business-related needs.

*   Build a common learning experience throughout your entire global organization with our core-content areas, localized into 16 languages.

*   Join thousands of organizations using the All Access Pass to implement strategy, close operational gaps, increase sales, drive customer loyalty, and improve employee engagement.

To learn more, visit
FRANKLINCOVEY.COM or call **1-888-868-1776.**

FranklinCovey
THE ULTIMATE COMPETITIVE ADVANTAGE